C SKILLS

HAL LEONARD STUDENT PIANO LIBRARY

Scales, Patterns, and Improvs

Improvisations, Scales, I-IV-V7 Chords, and Arpeggios

T0071551

TABLE OF CONTENTS

To access audio visit:
www.halleonard.com/mylibrary
Enter Code
3579-6255-3038-7372

Book
ISBN 978-1-4234-4218-9

Book/Audio
ISBN 978-1-4234-4221-9

HAL·LEONARD®
CORPORATION
7777 W. BLUEMOUND RD. P.O. BOX 13819 MILWAUKEE, WI 53213

In Australia contact:
Hal Leonard Australia Pty. Ltd.
4 Lentara Court
Cheltenham, Victoria, 3192 Australia
Email: ausadmin@halleonard.com.au

Visit Hal Leonard Online at
www.halleonard.com

A NOTE TO STUDENTS

Scales, Patterns, and Improvs presents the building blocks of music: scales, cadences, and arpeggios. You will encounter them everywhere in music, so it pays to know how to play them!

IMPROVS IN RELATED MAJOR AND MINOR KEYS

Every major key has a related minor key that begins on the sixth step of the major scale. Place your L.H. in the major five-finger position and your R.H. in the related minor five-finger position and improvise a melody as your teacher or the audio plays an accompaniment.

SCALES

Tucking 1 under 3

When playing scales (R.H. ascending/L.H. descending), tuck your thumb under your third finger. As soon as you play your thumb, move fingers 2-3-4-5 to their new positions. Let your arm guide your fingers smoothly up and down the keyboard, keeping your wrist level as you play each scale.

Crossing 3 over 1

When playing scales (R.H. descending/ L.H. ascending), let your wrist and forearm follow through as you cross your third finger over your thumb. As soon as you play finger 3, move fingers 2-1 to their new positions. Let your arm guide your fingers smoothly up and down the keyboard, keeping your wrist level as you play each scale.

CADENCES

When moving from one chord to another, gently reach with the thumb or fifth finger to the outside chord tones. Pay close attention to the finger playing the middle chord tone to maintain a comfortable hand position.

ARPEGGIOS

The arpeggio pattern covers the range of an octave. Gently extend your reach to cover the wider intervals, flexing your wrist gently from side to side as you play and release each key. Let your arm follow your fingers.

ETUDES

Put it all together! Play the folk song or etude for each key. Learn the additional skills of transposing, creating an accompaniment and playing from a lead line.

Best Wishes!

Barbara Kreader   Fred Kern   Phillip Keveren   Mona Rejino

UNIT 1 — C MAJOR–A MINOR

RELATED MAJOR AND MINOR PATTERNS – C MAJOR AND A MINOR

Every major five-finger pattern has a related minor five-finger pattern.

To find the related minor pattern:

1. Play the major pattern with your L.H.
2. Place your R.H. thumb one whole step above the highest note of the major pattern.
3. Play the minor pattern with your R.H.

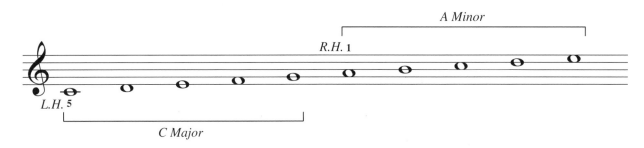

IMPROVISATION (IMPROV) IN C MAJOR AND A MINOR

As you listen to the accompaniment, improvise a melody beginning with the C Major pattern with your L.H. and moving to the A Minor pattern with your R.H. Your ear will tell you when to change to the A Minor pattern.

Accompaniment (Student improvises one octave higher than shown above.)

 TRACK 1

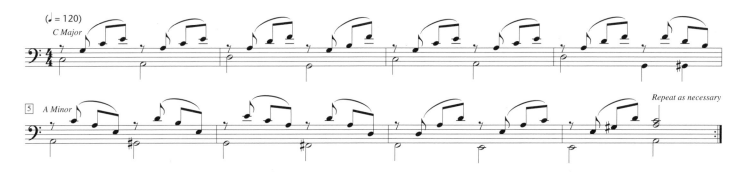

RELATED SCALES, CADENCES AND ARPEGGIOS

The **Key Signature** tells you which notes to play sharp or flat throughout the scale, cadence or arpeggio. The **Relative Keys** of C Major and A Minor have no sharps or flats.

Play the scales and chords hands separately before playing them hands together.

 TRACK 2

C MAJOR SCALE

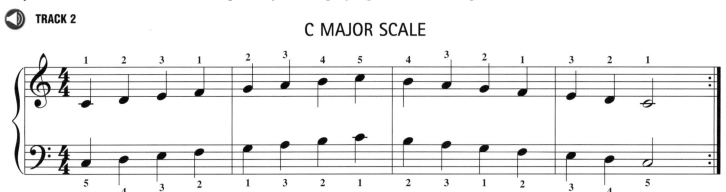

C MAJOR CADENCE

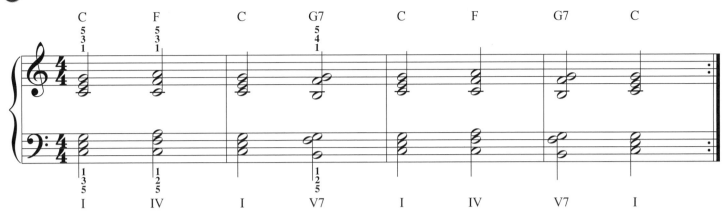

C MAJOR ARPEGGIO

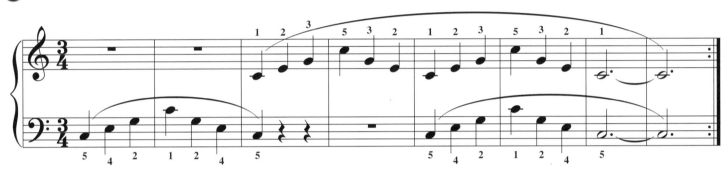

A MINOR SCALES

Natural Minor

The *Natural Minor* scale shares the same key signature with its *Relative Major*.

Harmonic Minor

The *Harmonic Minor* scale raises the 7th step.

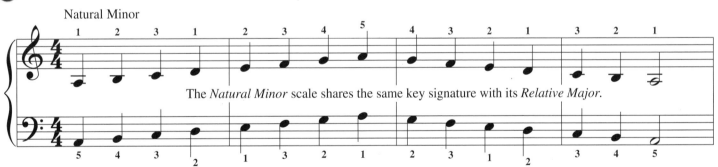
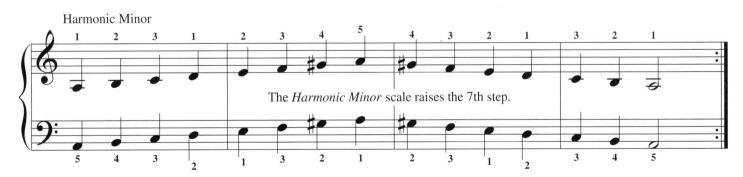

A MINOR CADENCE

TRACK 6

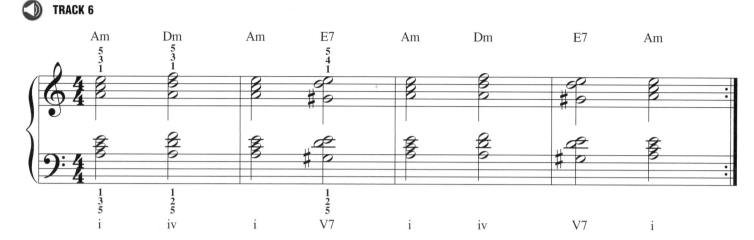

A MINOR ARPEGGIO

TRACK 7

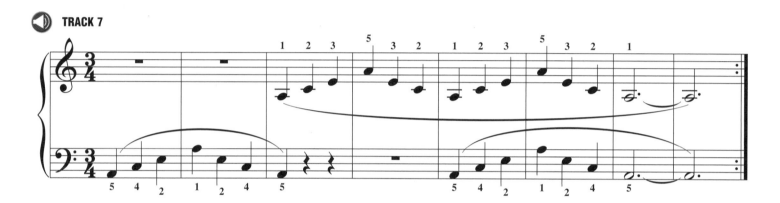

PATTERNS

When learning a new piece of music, it helps to find and identify the PATTERNS—scales, cadences, and arpeggios—the composer uses. The good news is that you already know how to play them!

Steps Before Reading and Playing *Waterslide*

1. Observe the clef signs and find where to place your hands.
2. Notice the meter and rhythm; review how to count it.
3. Identify the pattern that appears in measures 1-4. Is it a scale, cadence or arpeggio?
4. Identify the pattern that appears in measures 9-12. Is it a scale, cadence or arpeggio?
5. Identify the pattern that appears in measures 19-21. Is it a scale, cadence or arpeggio?
6. Count two measures in a moderate tempo before you begin.

WATERSLIDE

TRACK 8

Phillip Keveren

G MAJOR–E MINOR

RELATED MAJOR AND MINOR PATTERNS – G MAJOR AND E MINOR

Every major five-finger pattern has a related minor five-finger pattern.

To find the related minor pattern:

1. Play the major pattern with your L.H.
2. Place your R.H. thumb one whole step above the highest note of the major pattern.
3. Play the minor pattern with your R.H.

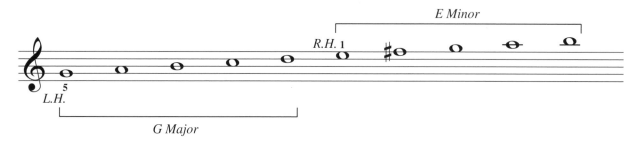

IMPROVISATION (IMPROV) IN G MAJOR AND E MINOR

As you listen to the accompaniment, improvise a melody beginning with the G Major pattern with your L.H. and moving to the E Minor pattern with your R.H. Your ear will tell you when to change to the E Minor pattern.

Accompaniment (Student improvises one octave higher than shown above.)

 TRACK 9

RELATED SCALES, CADENCES AND ARPEGGIOS

The **Key Signature** tells you which notes to play sharp or flat throughout the scale, cadence or arpeggio.
The **Relative Keys** of G Major and E Minor have one sharp, F♯.

G MAJOR SCALE

 TRACK 10

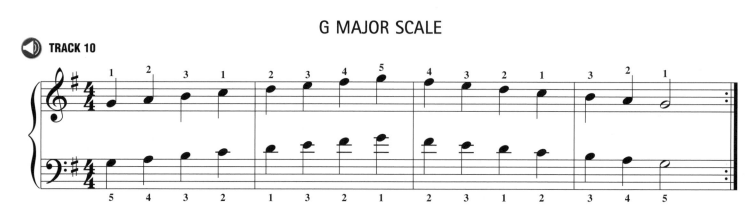

8

G MAJOR CADENCE

TRACK 11

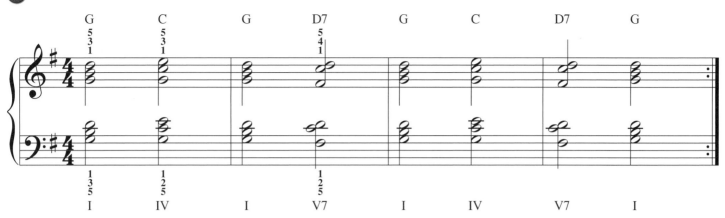

G MAJOR ARPEGGIO

TRACK 12

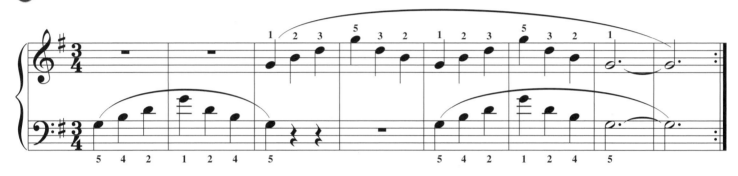

E MINOR SCALES

TRACK 13

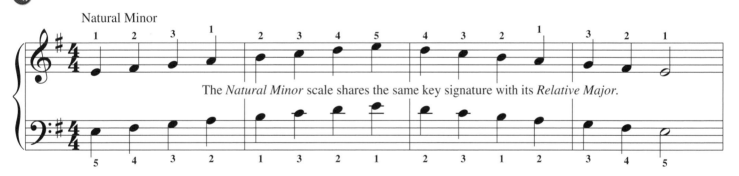

Natural Minor

The *Natural Minor* scale shares the same key signature with its *Relative Major*.

Harmonic Minor

The *Harmonic Minor* scale raises the 7th step.

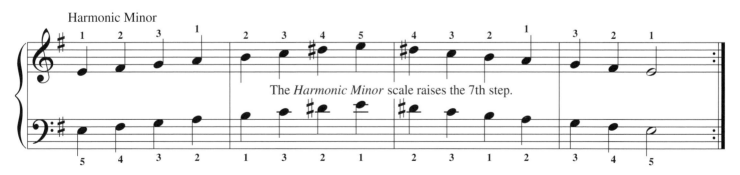

E MINOR CADENCE

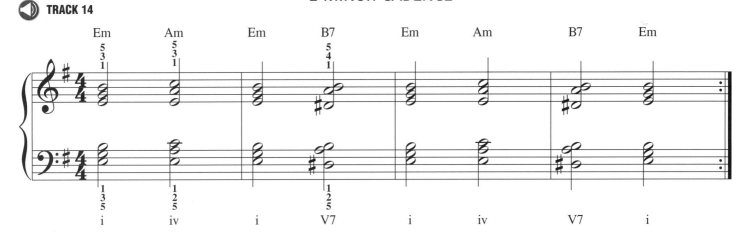

E MINOR ARPEGGIO

LEAD LINES

A **Lead Line** of a piece consists of the melody and the chords written in letters above the tune.

1. Play the right-hand melody of *French Folk Song*.
2. Practice the G Major Cadence chords on page 9.
3. Create an accompaniment with your left hand using the chord symbols above the melody.
4. Combine the right-hand melody with the left-hand accompaniment and play *French Folk Song*.

FRENCH FOLK SONG

French Folk Song

TRACK 16

D MAJOR–B MINOR

RELATED MAJOR AND MINOR PATTERNS – D MAJOR AND B MINOR

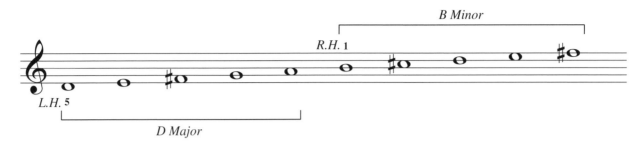

IMPROVISATION (IMPROV) IN D MAJOR AND B MINOR

As you listen to the accompaniment, improvise a melody beginning with the D Major pattern with your L.H. and moving to the B Minor pattern with your R.H. Your ear will tell you when to change to the B Minor pattern.

Accompaniment (Student improvises one octave higher than shown above.)

🔊 **TRACK 17**

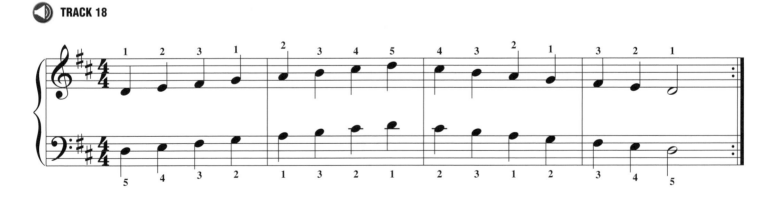

RELATED SCALES, CADENCES AND ARPEGGIOS

D MAJOR SCALE

🔊 **TRACK 18**

D MAJOR CADENCE

TRACK 19

D MAJOR ARPEGGIO

TRACK 20

B MINOR SCALES

TRACK 21

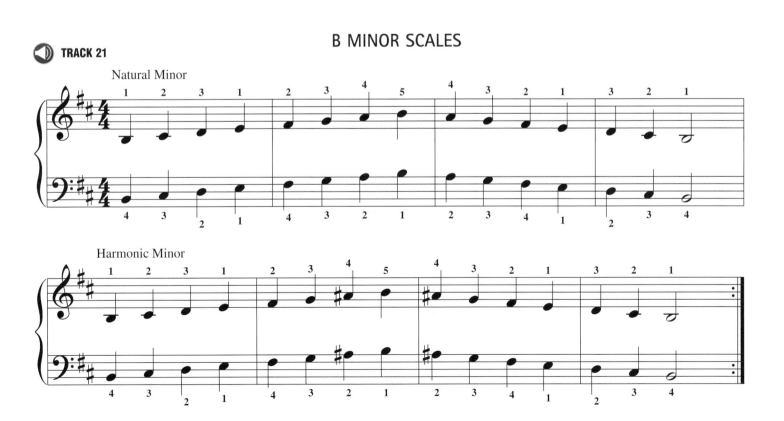

Natural Minor

Harmonic Minor

B MINOR CADENCE

TRACK 22

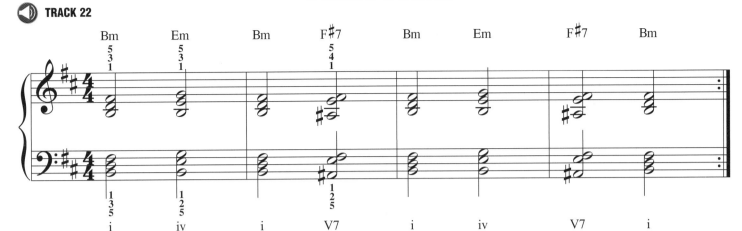

B MINOR ARPEGGIO

TRACK 23

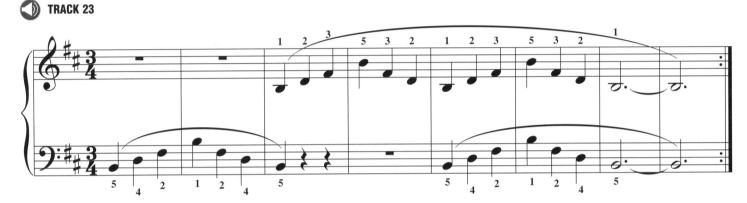

PATTERNS

Steps Before Reading and Playing *"You Don't Say!"*

1. Observe the clef signs and find where to place your hands.

2. Notice the meter and rhythm; review how to count it.

3. Identify the pattern that appears in the left hand in measures 1-2, 17-18, 21-22, 25-26, and 27-28. Is it a scale, cadence or arpeggio?

4. Identify the partial pattern that appears in the right hand in measures 2-4 and 18-20. Is it part of a scale, cadence or arpeggio?

5. Identify the pattern that appears in measures 6-8 and 22-24. Is it a scale, cadence or arpeggio?

6. Count two measures in a moderate tempo before you begin.

"YOU DON'T SAY!"

TRACK 24

Phillip Keveren

A MAJOR-F# MINOR

RELATED MAJOR AND MINOR PATTERNS – A MAJOR AND F# MINOR

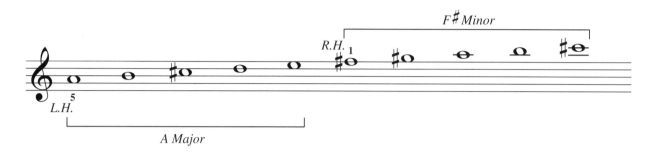

IMPROVISATION (IMPROV) IN A MAJOR AND F# MINOR

As you listen to the accompaniment, improvise a melody beginning with the A Major pattern with your L.H. and moving to the F# Minor pattern with your R.H. Your ear will tell you when to change to the F# Minor pattern.

Accompaniment (Student improvises one octave higher than shown above.)

TRACK 25

RELATED SCALES, CADENCES AND ARPEGGIOS

A MAJOR SCALE

TRACK 26

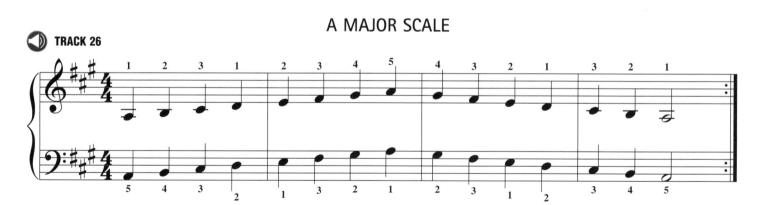

A MAJOR CADENCE

TRACK 27

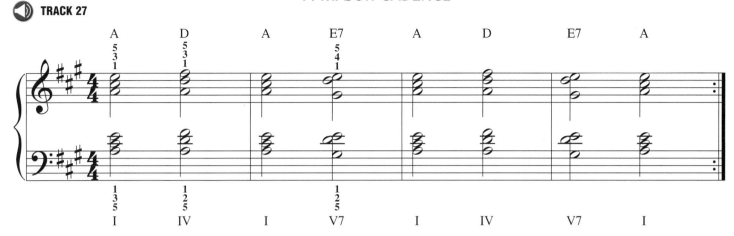

A MAJOR ARPEGGIO

TRACK 28

F# MINOR SCALES

TRACK 29

Natural Minor

Harmonic Minor

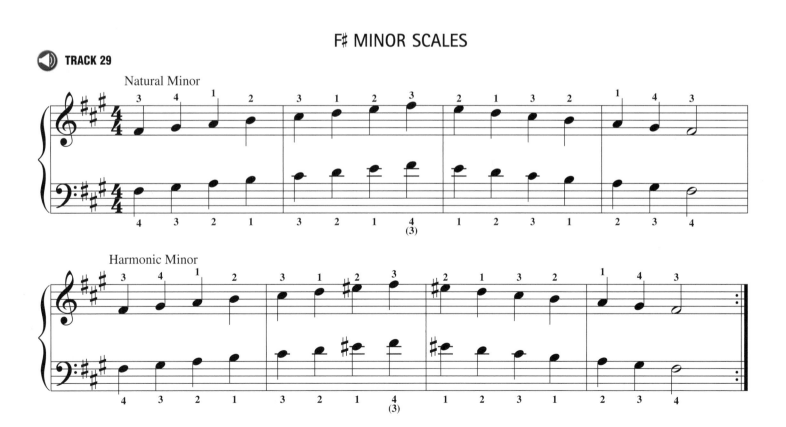

F♯ MINOR CADENCE

TRACK 30

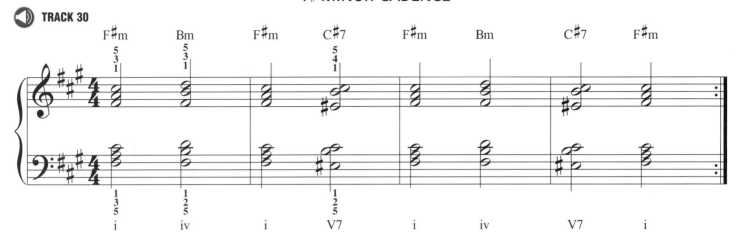

F♯ MINOR ARPEGGIO

TRACK 31

READING AND TRANSPOSING

Play *Polonaise*. Notice that measures 1-8 are in A Major and that measures 9-16 are in the **Relative Minor**, F♯ Minor.

POLONAISE

Anton Diabelli
adapted by Fred Kern

TRACK 32

Lively (♩ = 160)

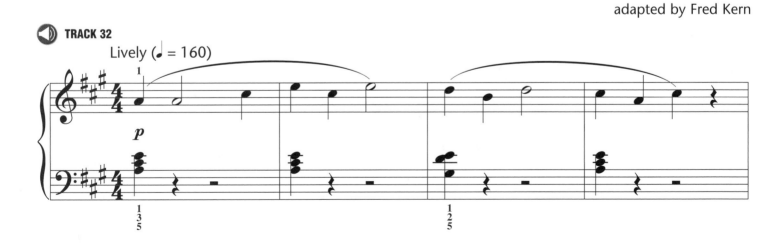

Transpose the first eight measures of *Polonaise* by playing the piece in G Major.

Keep the rhythms and intervals the same.

E MAJOR-C♯ MINOR

RELATED MAJOR AND MINOR PATTERNS - E MAJOR AND C♯ MINOR

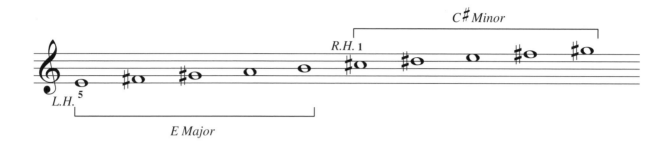

IMPROVISATION (IMPROV) IN E MAJOR AND C♯ MINOR

As you listen to the accompaniment, improvise a melody beginning with the E Major pattern with your L.H. and moving to the C♯ Minor pattern with your R.H. Your ear will tell you when to change to the C♯ Minor pattern.

Accompaniment (Student improvises one octave higher than shown above.)

🔊 **TRACK 33**

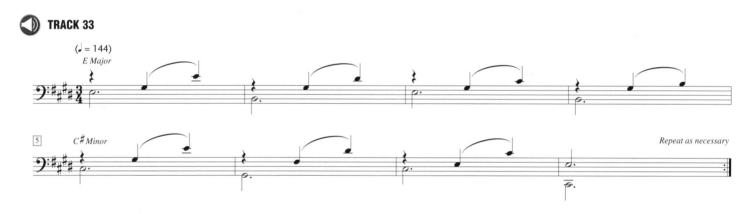

RELATED SCALES, CADENCE AND ARPEGGIOS

E MAJOR SCALE

🔊 **TRACK 34**

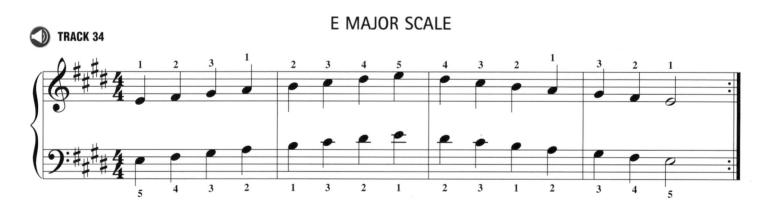

E MAJOR CADENCE

TRACK 35

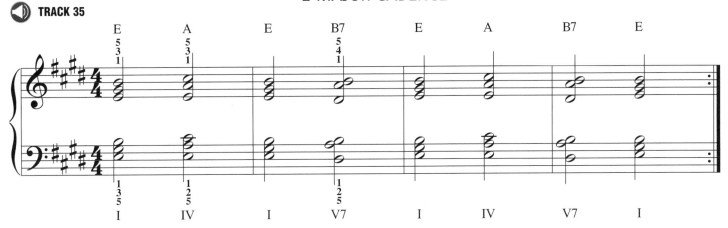

E MAJOR ARPEGGIO

TRACK 36

C♯ MINOR SCALES

TRACK 37

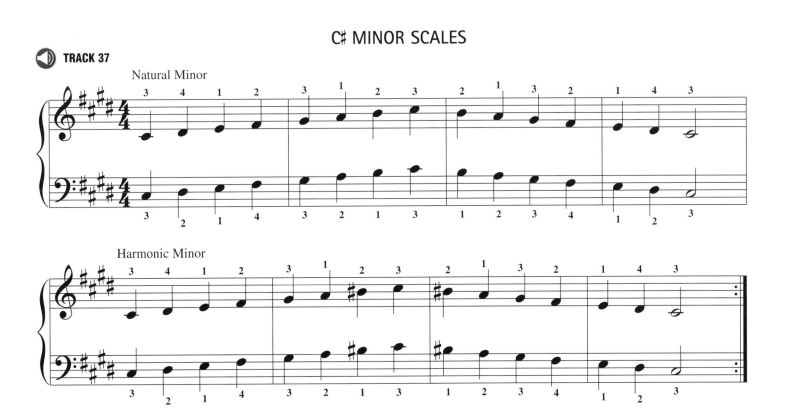

C♯ MINOR CADENCE

TRACK 38

C♯ MINOR ARPEGGIO

TRACK 39

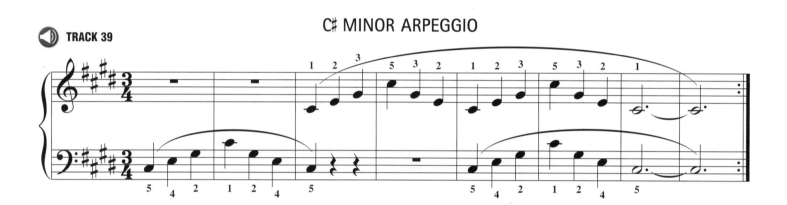

PATTERNS

Steps Before Reading and Playing *Evening Stroll*

1. Observe the clef signs and find where to place your hands.

2. Notice the meter and rhythm; review how to count it.

3. Identify the pattern that appears in the left hand in measures 1-6 and in measures 13-18. Is it a scale, cadence or arpeggio?

4. Identify the partial pattern that appears in the right hand in measures 8-11. Is it part of a scale, cadence or arpeggio?

5. Identify the pattern that appears in the last measure. Is it a scale, cadence or arpeggio?

6. Count two measures in a moderate tempo before you begin.

EVENING STROLL

TRACK 40

Phillip Keveren

UNIT 2   F MAJOR–D MINOR

RELATED MAJOR AND MINOR PATTERNS – F MAJOR AND D MINOR

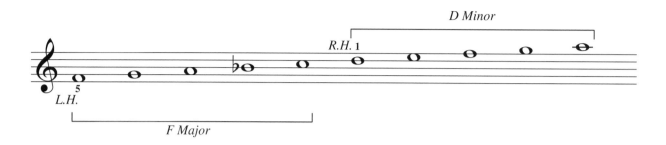

IMPROVISATION (IMPROV) IN F MAJOR AND D MINOR

As you listen to the accompaniment, improvise a melody beginning with the F Major pattern with your L.H. and moving to the D Minor pattern with your R.H. Your ear will tell you when to change to the D Minor pattern.

Accompaniment (Student improvises one octave higher than shown above.)

TRACK 41

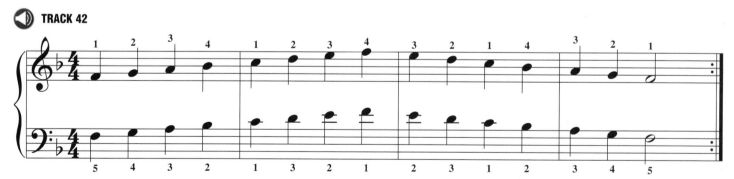

RELATED SCALES, CADENCES AND ARPEGGIOS

F MAJOR SCALE

TRACK 42

F MAJOR CADENCE

TRACK 43

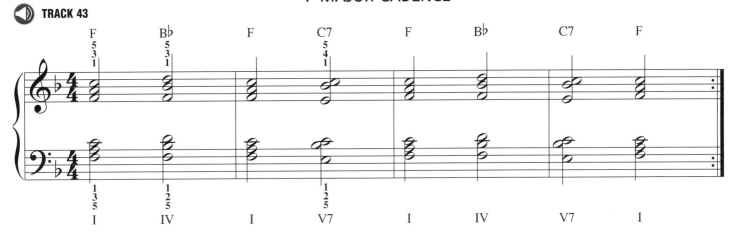

F MAJOR ARPEGGIO

TRACK 44

D MINOR SCALES

TRACK 45

Natural Minor

Harmonic Minor

D MINOR CADENCE

TRACK 46

D MINOR ARPEGGIO

TRACK 47

CHORDAL ACCOMPANIMENTS

1. Play the melody of *My Bonnie Lies Over the Ocean*.

2. Using the Roman numerals as a guide, write the correct I (F), IV (B♭), and V7 (C7) chords in the key of F Major in dotted half notes in the gray boxes.

3. Combine the melody with the accompaniment and play *My Bonnie Lies Over the Ocean*.

MY BONNIE LIES OVER THE OCEAN

TRACK 48

Scottish Folk Tune

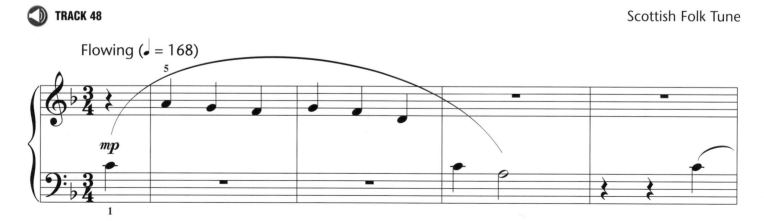

Bb MAJOR-G MINOR

RELATED MAJOR AND MINOR PATTERNS – Bb MAJOR AND G MINOR

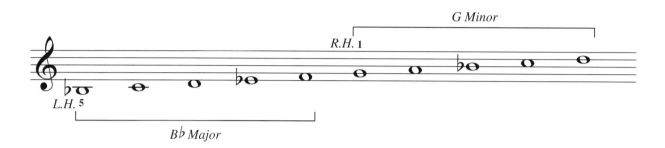

IMPROVISATION (IMPROV) IN Bb MAJOR AND G MINOR

As you listen to the accompaniment, improvise a melody beginning with the Bb Major pattern with your L.H. and moving to the G Minor pattern with your R.H. Your ear will tell you when to change to the G Minor pattern.

Accompaniment (Student improvises one octave higher than shown above.)

TRACK 49

RELATED SCALES, CADENCES AND ARPEGGIOS

Bb MAJOR SCALE

TRACK 50

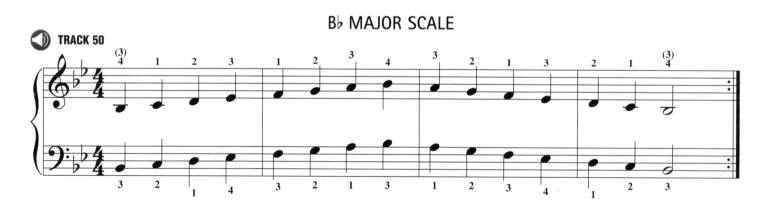

Bb MAJOR CADENCE

TRACK 51

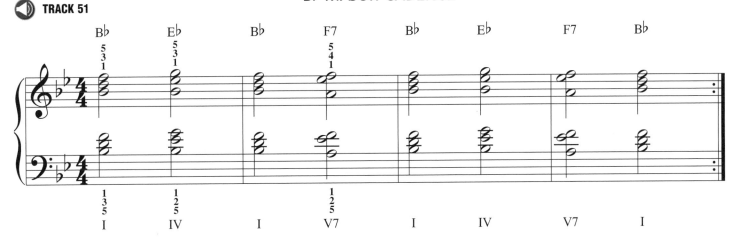

Bb MAJOR ARPEGGIO

TRACK 52

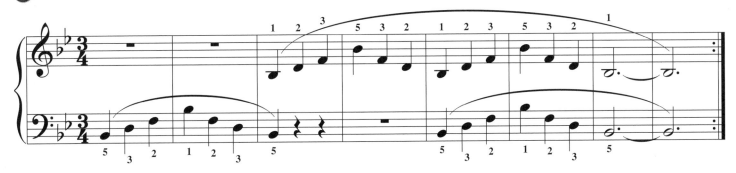

G MINOR SCALES

TRACK 53

Natural Minor

Harmonic Minor

G MINOR CADENCE

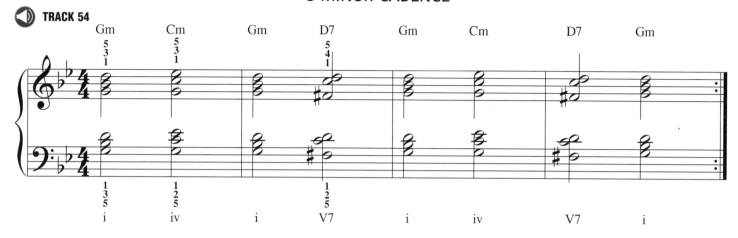

G MINOR ARPEGGIO

LEAD LINES

1. Play the right-hand melody of *Wayfaring Stranger*.

2. Practice the G Minor cadence chords indicated above the melody.

3. Create an accompaniment with your left hand using the chord symbols above the melody.

4. Combine the right-hand melody with the left-hand accompaniment and play *Wayfaring Stranger*.

WAYFARING STRANGER

Spiritual

Moderato (♩ = 120)

E♭ MAJOR–C MINOR

RELATED MAJOR AND MINOR PATTERNS – E♭ MAJOR AND C MINOR

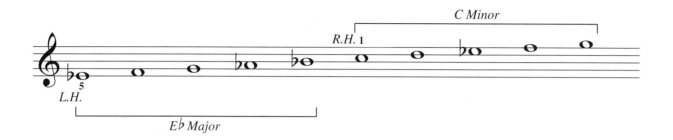

IMPROVISATION (IMPROV) IN E♭ MAJOR AND C MINOR

As you listen to the accompaniment, improvise a melody beginning with the E♭ Major pattern with your L.H. and moving to the C Minor pattern with your R.H. Your ear will tell you when to change to the C Minor pattern.

Accompaniment (Student improvises one octave higher than shown above.)

🔊 **TRACK 57**

RELATED SCALES, CADENCES AND ARPEGGIOS

E♭ MAJOR SCALE

🔊 **TRACK 58**

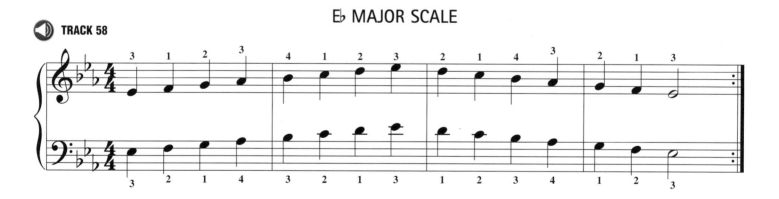

E♭ MAJOR CADENCE

TRACK 59

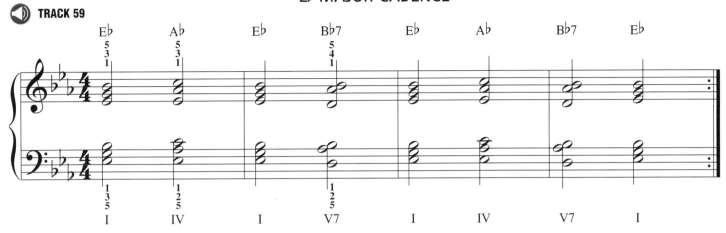

E♭ MAJOR ARPEGGIO

TRACK 60

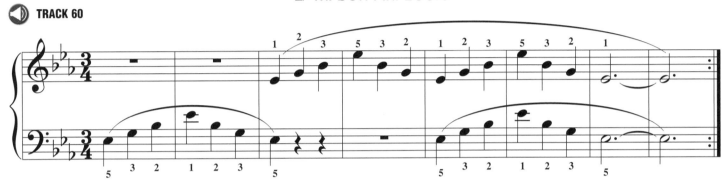

C MINOR SCALES

TRACK 61

Natural Minor

Harmonic Minor

C MINOR CADENCE

TRACK 62

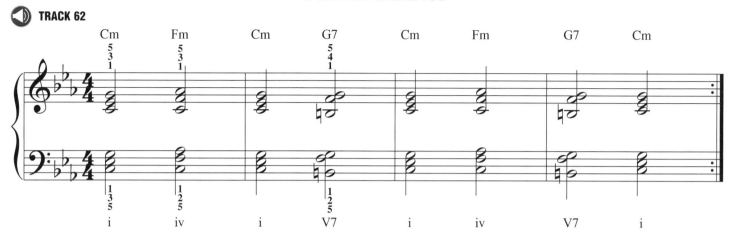

C MINOR ARPEGGIO

TRACK 63

READING AND TRANSPOSING

Play *March*. Notice that your left hand moves to the relative major chord pattern in measure 9 and returns to C minor in measure 17.

MARCH

Anton Diabelli
Adapted by Fred Kern

TRACK 64

Tempo di marcia (= 160)

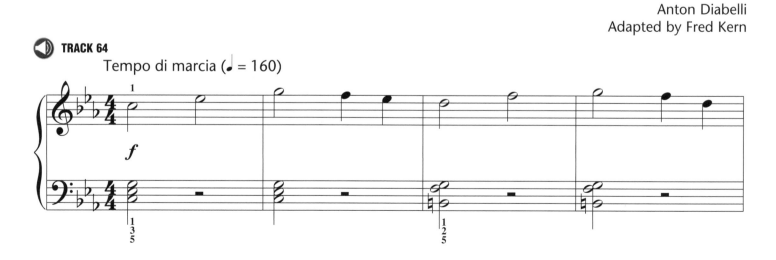

Transpose the first eight measures of *March* by playing the piece in D Minor. Keep the rhythms and intervals the same.

A♭ MAJOR–F MINOR

RELATED MAJOR AND MINOR PATTERNS – A♭ MAJOR AND F MINOR

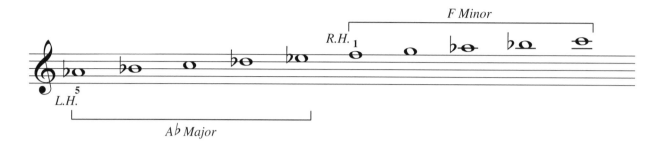

IMPROVISATION (IMPROV) IN A♭ MAJOR AND F MINOR

As you listen to the accompaniment, improvise a melody beginning with the A♭ Major pattern with your L.H. and moving to the F Minor pattern with your R.H. Your ear will tell you when to change to the F Minor pattern.

Accompaniment (Student improvises one octave higher than shown above.)

🔊 **TRACK 65**

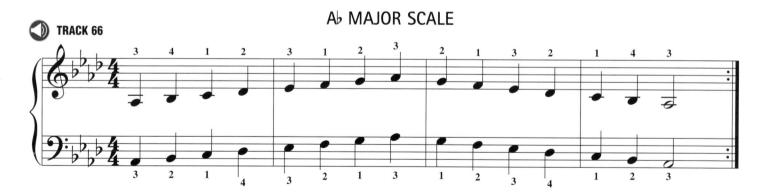

RELATED SCALES, CADENCES AND ARPEGGIOS

A♭ MAJOR SCALE

🔊 **TRACK 66**

A♭ MAJOR CADENCE

TRACK 67

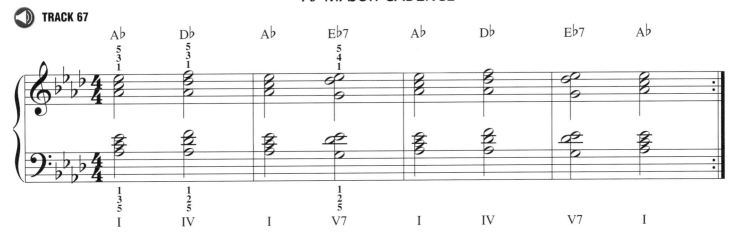

A♭ MAJOR ARPEGGIO

TRACK 68

F MINOR SCALES

TRACK 69

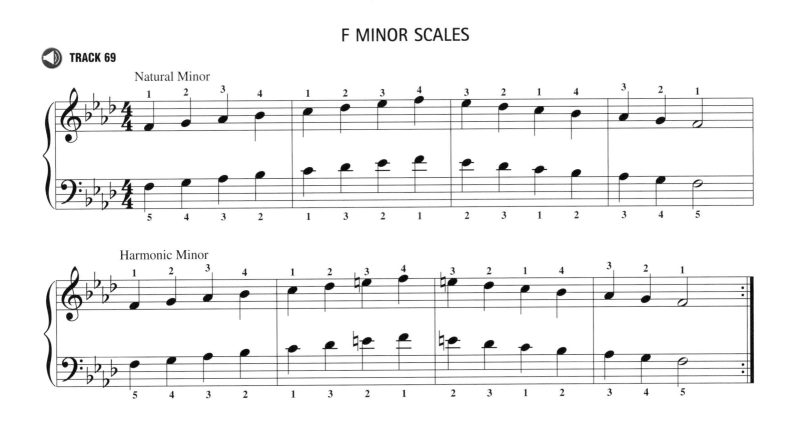

Natural Minor

Harmonic Minor

F MINOR CADENCE

TRACK 70

F MINOR ARPEGGIO

TRACK 71

CHORDAL ACCOMPANIMENTS

1. Play the melody of *Joshua Fit the Battle of Jericho*.

2. Using the Roman numerals as a guide, write the correct i, iv and V7 chords in the gray boxes. Use quarter notes in measures 8 and 9. Use whole notes in the remaining measures.

3. Combine the melody with the accompaniment and play *Joshua Fit the Battle of Jericho*.

JOSHUA FIT THE BATTLE OF JERICHO

Spiritual

TRACK 72

Allegro (♩ = 132)

UNIT 3 — Dь MAJOR–Bь MINOR

RELATED SCALES, CADENCES AND ARPEGGIOS

Dь MAJOR SCALE

TRACK 73

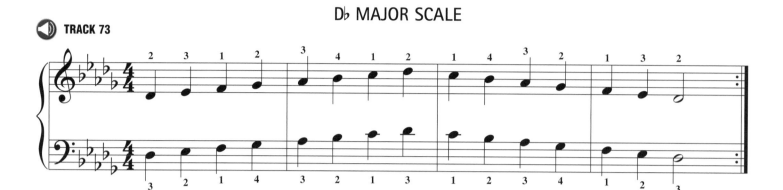

Dь MAJOR CADENCE

TRACK 74

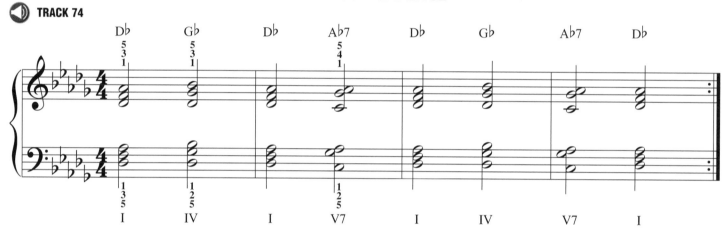

Dь MAJOR ARPEGGIO

TRACK 75

B♭ MINOR SCALES

TRACK 76

Natural Minor

Harmonic Minor

B♭ MINOR CADENCE

TRACK 77

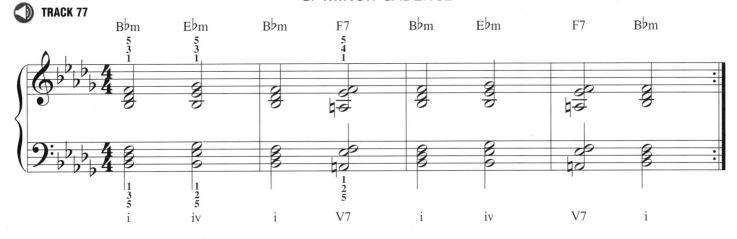

B♭m   E♭m   B♭m   F7   B♭m   E♭m   F7   B♭m

i   iv   i   V7   i   iv   V7   i

B♭ MINOR ARPEGGIO

TRACK 78

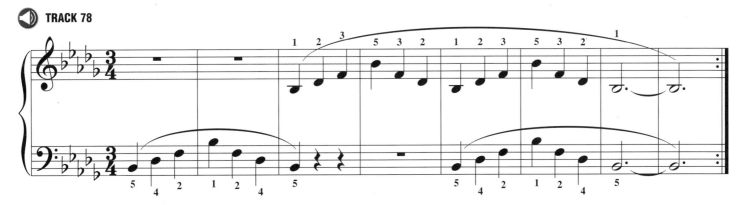

G♭ MAJOR-E♭ MINOR

RELATED SCALES, CADENCES AND ARPEGGIOS

G♭ MAJOR SCALE

TRACK 79

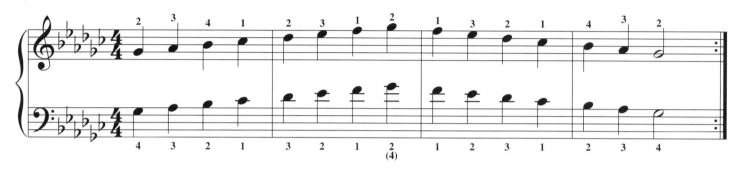

G♭ MAJOR CADENCE

TRACK 80

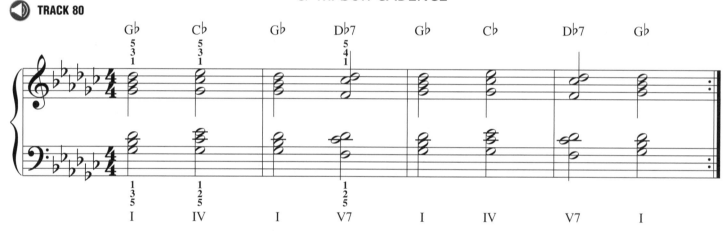

G♭ MAJOR ARPEGGIO

TRACK 81

E♭ MINOR SCALES

TRACK 82

Natural Minor

Harmonic Minor

E♭ MINOR CADENCE

TRACK 83

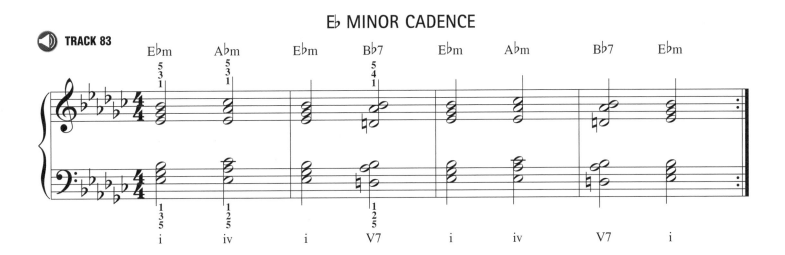

E♭m   A♭m   E♭m   B♭7   E♭m   A♭m   B♭7   E♭m

i   iv   i   V7   i   iv   V7   i

E♭ MINOR ARPEGGIO

TRACK 84

B MAJOR-G♯ MINOR

RELATED SCALES, CADENCES AND ARPEGGIOS

B MAJOR SCALE

TRACK 85

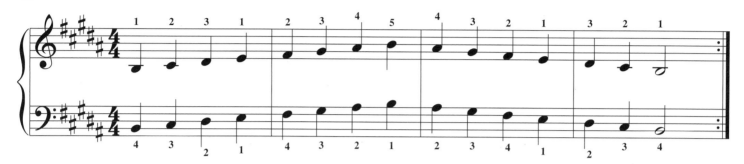

B MAJOR CADENCE

TRACK 86

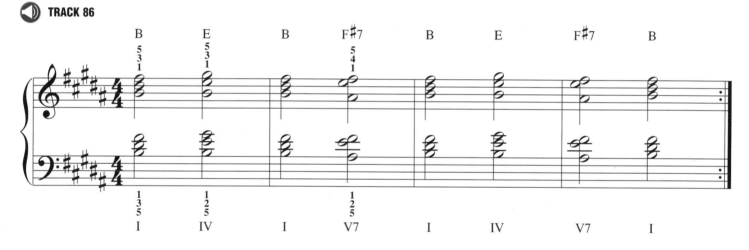

B MAJOR ARPEGGIO

TRACK 87

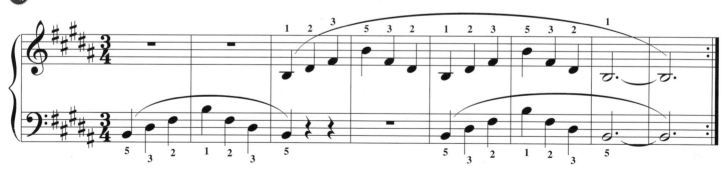

G♯ MINOR SCALES

TRACK 88

Natural Minor

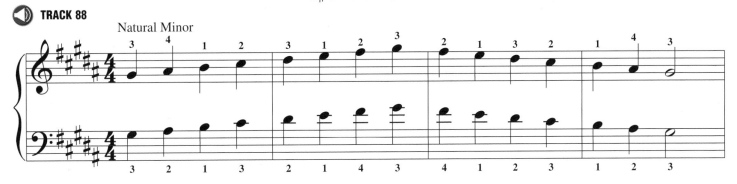

Harmonic Minor

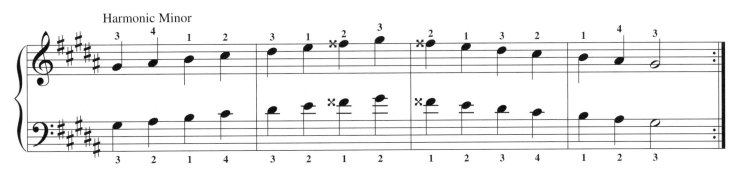

G♯ MINOR CADENCE

TRACK 89

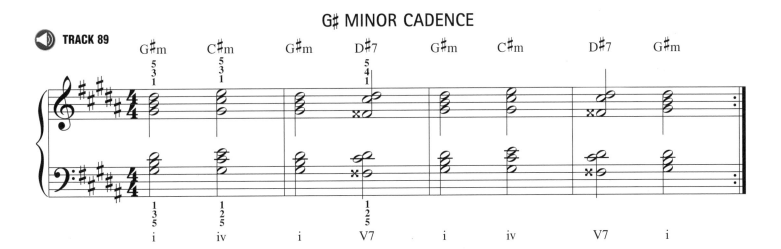

G♯ MINOR ARPEGGIO

TRACK 90

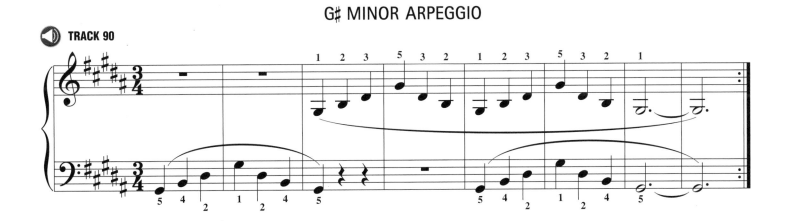

CIRCLE OF FIFTHS

Now that you know how to improvise and play scales, cadences and arpeggios in all keys, it is time to put the major keys together to make harmonic progressions. Begin with C and move clockwise around the Circle of Fifths. Learn to play this Circle of Fifths progression by memory. Once your fingers know these harmonic progressions, you will be ready to create more complex improvisations.

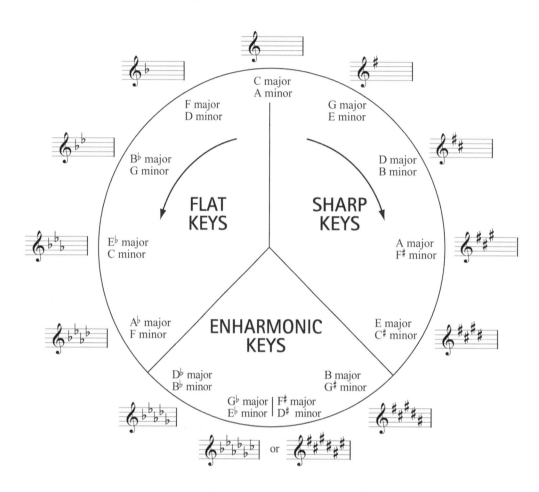

TRACK 91

CIRCLE OF FIFTHS ETUDE

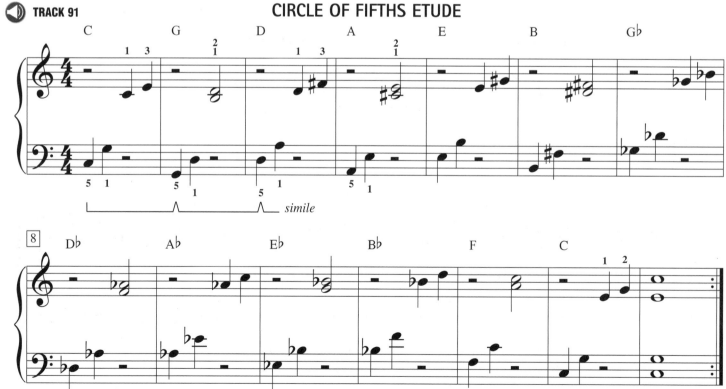

CIRCLE OF FOURTHS

Begin with C and play counterclockwise around the Circle of Fourths. Memorize this progression and you will have even more building blocks in your musical vocabulary.

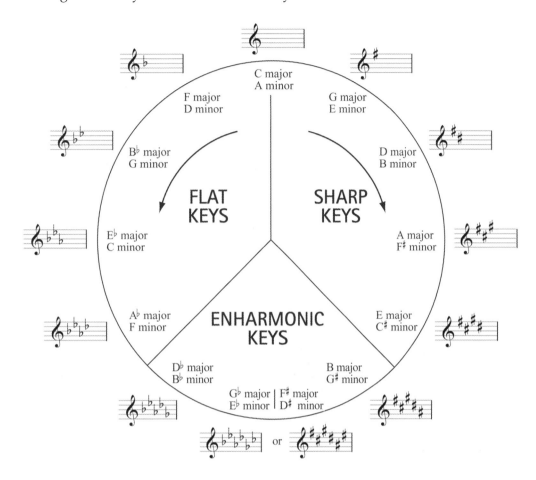

CIRCLE OF FOURTHS ETUDE

TRACK 92